Classroom Management Through Curricular Adaptations

Educating Minority Handicapped Students

John J. Hoover

Catherine Collier

Hamilton Publications
Lindale, Texas

ISBN 0-940059-00-2

Library of Congress Catalog Card Number: 86-82580

Contents

Preface

Teachers are currently faced with the unparalleled challenge of educating minority handicapped students who exhibit learning and behavior problems. Within the framework of providing appropriate education to these learners, overall effective classroom management is vital. As we view the management of the total classroom environment the curriculum (and its different elements) must be considered. The curriculum and its appropriate implementation are critical to effective class management. In this respect, effective classroom management for minority handicapped students is a direct function of effective curriculum implementation, as well as adaptations that may be necessary to meet the learning and behavior problems these students bring to the classroom situation.

This book explores classroom management for minority handicapped students. Emphasized within this book is the position that effective classroom management for minority handicapped students is best achieved as curriculum is appropriately adapted to meet the specific needs that these special learners bring to the classroom. Various aspects of curriculum in addition to content will be explored. The other curriculum areas that must be addressed when considering classroom management are instructional strategies, class instructional settings, student behaviors, and the integration of these curriculum aspects within the total classroom environment.

This book is written primarily for teachers who are faced with the seemingly insurmountable task of educating minority handicapped students. The model for classroom management explored in the chapters of this book is designed to provide the reader a practical framework within which a more complete understanding of specific problems of minority handicapped students can be viewed. Also discussed are numerous teaching techniques to provide effective intervention and remediation pertaining to the interrelated areas of classroom management and curriculum. The authors wish to express their appreciation to the professionals who reviewed this manuscript at various stages of development. Their insightful suggestions and criticisms contributed to the conceptualization of the concepts presented in this book.

J.J.H.
C.C.

Chapter 1
Introduction to Curriculum and Class Management

A central element of classroom instruction is obviously the curriculum. Everything that we as educators elect to teach, as well as choose not to teach, eventually affects the curriculum. Thus, how curriculum is defined directly affects what occurs in our classrooms. Additionally, the confounding variables of state and local legislation, parental pressures, or administrative mandates all influence the curriculum we implement in our classrooms.

Interrelated within the curriculum in any classroom is the total classroom management system one employs. The specific teaching and behavior management strategies used to implement curriculum content, manage behavior, and in general organize classroom instruction, assist in determining not only the total curriculum but also the total class management. In this respect, classroom management and the curriculum are two interrelated and inseparable aspects of the total educational process.

This chapter explores the interrelationship between curriculum and classroom management. It will begin by exploring the various elements found within the elusive term known as "curriculum." It will then discuss classroom management and explore the concept that, in actual practice, effective classroom management for minority handicapped students is the same as effective curriculum implementation.

Curriculum Defined

According to Wiles and Bondi (1984), the predominant trend or theme in a continually evolving definition of curriculum defines curriculum as all planned and guided learning experiences under the direction of the school. These experiences should have intended educational consequences (Eisner, 1979). Since this and similar broad definitions of curriculum are frequently used by curriculum specialists as well as other educators (Doll, 1978; Lemlech, 1984; Tanner and Tanner, 1975), this definition will be adhered to when the general term "curriculum" is used throughout this book. Although a general definition of curriculum is accepted and understood by most classroom teachers, the specific aspects that comprise curriculum are not as clear. Indeed, to many educators the curriculum is merely the book or books we use in our classrooms. Otherwise known as content, this curricular element is only one important element in the total curriculum process.

Elements Comprising Curriculum

Four major elements comprise curriculum. These include the content that is taught, the instructional strategies, classroom instructional settings, and student behaviors. Each of these four major areas within the total curriculum must be understood relative to their relationship with each other as well as to individual student needs, cultural heritages, and prior experiences.

The element of content refers to the academic skills and knowledge associated with the various subject areas. In today's schools this is frequently a developmentally and sequentially-ordered program. This element includes prerequisite skills needed to complete academic tasks as well as expressive and receptive language skills necessary to comprehend and learn the content. The instructional strategies are the methods and techniques selected to assist students to acquire the content as well as manage behavior. The instructional settings refer to the settings in the classroom in which learning occurs. These include small and large group situations as well as independent work and one-to-one instructional situations. The student behaviors aspect of the total curriculum refers to the minority handicapped students' abilities to manage and control their own behaviors under a variety of situations, learning activities, and groupings within the classroom.

3

All of these four elements of the total curriculum are individual factors that contribute to the success of education for minority handicapped students. Although the authors contend that these four elements are distinct aspects of the total curriculum, the interrelationship among these elements provides the key to success when the total curriculum is implemented.

Problems, inconsistencies, and other events within a classroom that inhibit effective implementation of curriculum are frequently the result of problems associated with two or more of these curriculum elements. Although a problem limited to only one element of the curriculum is sometimes encountered, many minority handicapped students who experience problems within the classroom are having difficulty in more than one element within the total curriculum. However, all too often we concentrate our search for and/or solutions to academic and behavior problems within the individual elements without thinking through the possible interrelationships among the various elements.

By ignoring the interrelationship among the elements we frequently embark upon a path designed to improve learning or reduce behavior problems that is doomed to failure from the very beginning. All too often teachers find themselves saying that they were sure that the problem was "due to" one of the curriculum elements (i.e., content, strategies), and after spending several weeks modifying or focusing upon the individual area(s), they realized that something else is also contributing to the learning/behavior problems.

The authors believe that in many situations that "something else" pertains to the interrelationship among elements. As one element is addressed or adapted each of the other three elements may also be affected. Thus, as one curriculum element is adapted or modified, each of the other three areas must also be addressed to determine the effects of the original adaptations upon them, and if necessary, also adapted to address potential problems that may arise.

Interrelationship Among Curricular Elements

The crucial interrelationship between these curriculum elements and the curriculum implementation process is illustrated in Figure 1. As shown, the four curricular elements are identified on the outside borders of the figure. The center of the figure represents the curriculum implementation process which is achieved through each of the four elements. The areas within the figure describe important interrelationships among the different elements. For example, student behaviors influence and are influenced by the instructional strategies and classroom instructional settings. The area of content may influence the selection of the instructional strategies and class instructional settings used. Also, the instructional strategies may influence the type of instructional settings selected. The classroom instructional setting selected may influence the selection of instructional strategies and is influenced by student behaviors, as well as content to be learned. The following situations illustrate the interrelationship among curricular elements.

Situation 1:

Tony is a third grade student whose native language is Spanish, although he is capable of speaking and understanding English appropriate for his age and grade level. Tony is functioning academically at a first grade level in reading, and attends a special education resource room on a daily basis for reading and language instruction. In addition, he has difficulty working with other students, especially in small group situations.

Figure 1
Interrelationship Among Curricular Elements in the Curriculum Implementation Process

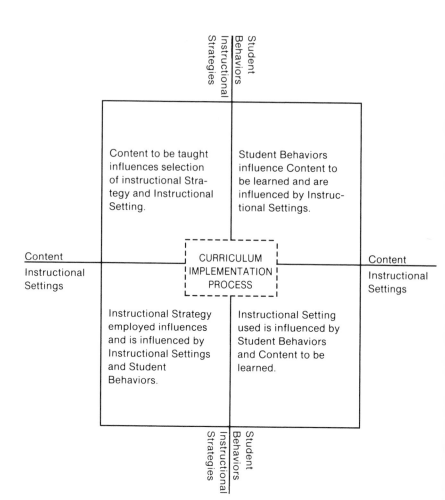

Specifically, Tony frequently bites and pokes other students while waiting his turn to answer a question or when others are responding to a question. You wish to teach Tony some first grade sight words. Several other students in the same class also need to learn the same sight words. You choose to present the sight words (content) on flash cards asking Tony to say each word (instructional strategy) in a one-to-one situation (instructional setting). In this situation, Tony's behavior influenced the instructional setting (i.e., one-to-one setting). Additionally, the instructional strategy (i.e., flash card presentation) was influenced by Tony's behavior as well as the content to be learned. If Tony was capable of working with others, a small group situation would have been selected, since others in the class required work on the same words.

Now suppose you decide to present the words in a small group setting, including Tony. Since Tony has difficulty waiting his turn, the strategy of asking each student to respond to the sight words on flash cards one at a time may not be in the best interest of Tony or the others in the group. Thus, by changing the instructional setting to a small group rather than one-to-one situation, the instructional strategy also requires change to meet both Tony's and the other students' abilities. Instead of showing the flash cards one at a time and asking each student to take turns responding, sight word bingo may be played. In this game, all students must respond to each flash card by placing an X on the sight word on their cards if it is the same as the word on the flash card.

The interrelationship among elements is very evident in this situation. By selecting the small group situation (i.e., instructional setting) the instructional strategy was directly influenced. As the instructional setting element was changed for Tony, the instructional strategy also required change. Thus, the instructional setting influenced

the instructional strategy, which was also
influenced by student (Tony's) behaviors.

Situation 2:

   Maria is a seventh grade Native American
student who speaks fluent Apache and some English.
She is functioning academically in reading and math
at about the fourth grade level, and is an extremely
shy, withdrawn girl. Maria was appropriately placed
into special education where she receives resource
room assistance on a daily basis for work on
academics and social/emotional development. Based
upon this information, you choose to teach Maria
some social and interpersonal relationship skills
(content) in small group and one-to-one situations
(instructional settings), through a bilingual peer
tutoring approach (instructional strategy). Academic
work is completed on an individual basis until Maria
feels more comfortable working in small groups.
   In this situation, Maria's behavior (student
behaviors) influenced the selection of content
(i.e., social skills development), the instructional
setting (i.e., small group; one-to-one), as well as
the instructional strategy (i.e., peer tutoring).
Also, the instructional strategy was influenced by
the content selected and the instructional setting
used.

   Thus, the implementation of curriculum in any
one classroom for minority handicapped students
involves much more than simply selecting a teaching
technique and teaching content. The management of
student behaviors cannot be fully realized unless
all aspects of the total curriculum are considered
in the decision making process. In this respect, the
decision to select and implement, change, modify, or
adapt one element within the total curriculum
process must be made relative to each of the other

three elements. Careful consideration prior to implementing curriculum for minority handicapped students will assist teachers to minimize failure and provide a greater chance for success by ensuring that each of the important areas within the curriculum has been addressed prior to implementing instruction.

Class Management and Curricular Elements

Lewis and Doorlag (1983) cited Stephens (1980) when defining classroom management. They wrote that class management refers to those things teachers do to facilitate a meaningful and safe classroom environment. This includes considering the various characteristics of the group of students, the physical classroom environment, availability and use of time, use of reinforcement, interactions among students and teachers, and individualization of instruction (Lewis and Doorlag, 1983). Stated differently, classroom management as used throughout this book is defined as the employment of teaching and behavior management techniques within a classroom situation that allow each student to individually, or in group situations, acquire knowledge and skills necessary for positive growth and development. This includes the areas of academics, social/emotional development, and physical development.

Based upon this definition, effective classroom management is perceived as the effective implementation of various teaching and behavior management techniques within appropriate classroom instructional settings which will allow each student to acquire knowledge and skills for positive growth in the areas of academics, social/emotional development, and physical development. Referring to the four curricular elements found within the curriculum implementation process we are able to see that effective classroom management also includes these same four areas. In this respect, effective

classroom management is effective implementation of
the total curriculum.

Figure 2 illustrates a model that depicts the
process of classroom management through curriculum
implementation. A circular figure is used to
illustrate the continuous interaction among the four
elements of curriculum comprising the curriculum
implementation process. As shown in the figure, the
four curriculum elements are first illustrated as
individual areas. These four elements connect to the
circular area depicting curriculum implementation,
which in turn connects with the inner most circle of
classroom management.

When educating minority handicapped students
all of the four curriculum elements are addressed,
first as individual components, and ultimately, as
interrelated elements. This represents the total
curriculum implementation process. As the four
curriculum elements are collectively and effectively
implemented (i.e., curriculum implementation
process), effective classroom management emerges.

As we consider factors associated with the four
elements of curriculum it is possible to further
define effective classroom management for minority
handicapped students. First, the academic content
one teaches to minority handicapped students must be
carefully selected. Factors such as prior
educational experiences, prior community and social
experiences, success within various content areas,
mastery of necessary prerequisite skills, and
current language skills must all be addressed and
considered prior to teaching minority handicapped
students specific content. When selecting content,
of greatest importance to teachers of these special
learners are prerequisite skills, prior educational
and social experiences, and current language
functioning within the English language. Thus, in
order to ensure effective classroom management when
teaching minority handicapped students, each of
these important content-related areas must be
considered.

Figure 2
Integrative Model for Classroom Management
and Curriculum Implementation

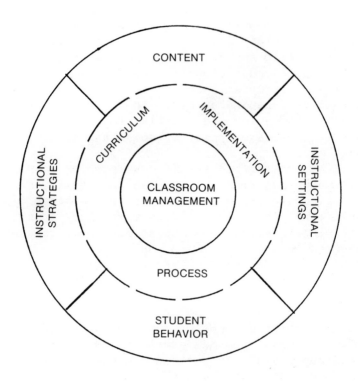

Once the specific content to be learned has been selected, the second element of instructional strategies is addressed. The strategies to be used to help the students acquire the knowledge and skills must now be determined. Although the content to be learned may influence the selection of strategies, in many situations the selection of strategies is based upon other factors in addition to the content to be studied.

When selecting strategies for implementing instruction to minority handicapped students, the teacher must consider several important factors. The strategies selected must, most importantly, allow the student to succeed at the task at hand. Factors such as prior educational successes and failures, acquired prerequisite skills, current receptive and expressive language skills, and difficulty of the material to be learned are also important areas that must be considered prior to selecting strategies for teaching.

The extent that specific strategies do not accommodate varying backgrounds and abilities limits the effectiveness of one's overall classroom management. Effective classroom management involves careful selection of the strategies used to assist students to not only learn content but also to acquire the skills necessary to manage their own behaviors. Thus, the selected strategies must ensure success with content as well as management of behavior.

The third element of curriculum that comprises effective classroom management for minority handicapped students pertains to the classroom instructional settings used to facilitate learning. The classroom instructional setting refers to the various groupings and independent seatwork situations often found in today's schools. These may include large group (entire class); small group; one-to-one instructional settings; work completed individually at tables, desks, or in centers located throughout the classroom; or, some combination of the above limited only by the creativity of each individual teacher.

Important within the total framework of effective classroom management is the idea that the selection of the classroom instructional setting requires careful decision making and thought. Equally important is the understanding that much content can be taught in a variety of classroom instructional settings. In addition, many different instructional strategies can be successfully implemented in different instructional settings.

Although influenced by content and/or instructional strategies, the decision to teach specific content and/or employ specific instructional strategies does not automatically lead to or require a specific type of classroom instructional setting. For example, use of a lecture-type technique may be employed in an individual, small group, or large group setting. Although this technique is typically used with larger groups of students, a teacher could use this method with an individual student. A similar example may be seen with the use of the method known as contingency contracting with students. The same specific contract may be implemented with a group of students or with an individual student. Although typically used with individual students, contracting is also appropriate in some situations for use with small or large groups of students.

When selecting the most appropriate classroom instructional setting for minority handicapped students one must consider several factors. The classroom instructional setting must show the students that they are expected to learn as well as complete the required tasks. It is very important that students perceive the setting as a forum that minimizes their risk for failure while it simultaneously conveys the message that they are expected to complete and learn the task at hand.

The teacher must also consider the students' prior educational successes and failures relative to grouping situations, the difficulty level of the material to be learned, the length of time required by the student to complete the task, the importance (for the specific task) of direct interaction between the teacher and student or student-student interaction, as well as the best classroom instructional setting necessary to implement the selected instructional strategy. By carefully weighing each of these factors as well as the other important areas discussed for the previous two elements, the best classroom instructional setting for each minority handicapped student can be determined.

The fourth curriculum element crucial to overall effective classroom management is the component of student behaviors. This element pertains to the learners' abilities to maintain and manage their own behaviors. Minority handicapped students' inability to manage their own behaviors often presents the greatest challenge to the classroom teacher. Deficit skills in this area of curriculum and classroom management will affect decisions related to the selection of instructional strategies, classroom instructional settings, and to some extent the type of content to be learned.

It is important for the teacher to examine whether the content being taught, the strategies employed to teach the content, and/or the type of classroom instructional settings used contribute to assisting minority handicapped students to manage and control their own behaviors. In some instances, the learners' inability to sufficiently control/manage their own behavior may permeate most content areas, many different strategies employed, and most classroom instructional settings. However, for other students, the inability to manage/control their own behavior may be linked directly to specific content (e.g., reading or math), certain types of instructional strategies, and limited to only one classroom instructional setting (e.g., small groups).

In either type of situation, careful consideration of student behaviors in the decision making process pertaining to content, strategies, and instructional settings will prove beneficial to both the teacher and the students in question. Many of the same factors that must be considered when selecting content, strategies, and instructional settings that have been discussed previously must also be considered as minority handicapped students encounter problems managing their own behaviors.

Interrelationship: Class Management and Curriculum Implementation

As shown in Figure 2 and based upon the definition and description of classroom management, it should be apparent that effective classroom management is a direct function of the effective implementation of the four interrelated elements comprising the total curriculum process. The extent that the four interrelated curriculum elements are not properly implemented directly affects one's classroom management. Kerr and Nelson (1983) wrote that the organization of curriculum, the daily structure and physical environment, arrangement of instruction, as well as the management of student behavior, all contribute to overall classroom management.

In looking at the definition of classroom management (i.e., effective implementation of the curriculum), it becomes very difficult to separate these two areas as instruction is delivered to minority handicapped students. The most positive learning environment for these special learners is one which promotes effective classroom management through the process of effective implementation of the total curriculum.

In order to best accomplish this goal for many minority handicapped students, curriculum as it is typically found within today's schools must frequently be modified or adapted to meet individual needs. If individual needs within a classroom are not being met, the overall classroom management requires modifications. In the next chapter we will discuss the specific needs of these special learners. Chapter 3 will discuss curricular adaptations which is the most productive means to achieving effective classroom management for minority handicapped students.

Chapter 2
Understanding the Minority Handicapped Student

To understand minority handicapped students one must consider the three interrelated elements of culture, language, and handicap. Knowledge about these special learners relative to these three areas will assist in providing the most effective classroom management through curriculum implementation. Each of these three areas is addressed in this chapter with specific emphasis placed upon issues important to consider within these areas when educating minority handicapped students.

Culture

Classroom instruction must be based upon knowledge of the specific culture, the learning needs of the students, as well as the goals and expectations of the local community. When using materials from particular resources and adapting materials from another cultural context, the teacher should be sensitive to the difficulties inherent in linguistic and cultural transference. The effects of acculturation, experiential differences, sociocultural factors, interaction patterns, discrimination, and cognitive and learning strategy differences are all important cultural factors that must be addressed when considering class management and curriculum implementation for minority handicapped students.

Acculturation

Acculturation, which may take many forms, is the process by which humans adapt to a new cultural environment. One of these is "assimilation" which refers to the native culture being replaced or submerged by a second culture. Another and more common form of acculturation is "integration" which refers to the maintenance of elements of the native culture while learning elements of a new culture. The result of integration is a blending of these elements from the native culture (C1) and the new cultural environment (C2) (Padilla, 1980). While students confront the acculturation process, they may experience difficulty benefiting fully from the special efforts designed to address their special needs. During early stages of the acculturation process, learners may not as yet possess the linguistic or cognitive tools necessary to fully grasp and expand upon classroom experiences. Only with early crosscultural intervention and assistance in the acculturation process will the students achieve and maintain a level commensurate with their abilities. Without specific intervention, some estimates suggest 5-7 years are necessary for a child exposed to a new language and culture to integrate the native and mainstream culture and the associated first and second languages (Cummins, 1981a).

Students going through the acculturation process may experience heightened anxiety, low self esteem, and confusion in internal vs external locus of control as part of this adaptation process (Adler, 1975; Juffer, 1983). These "side effects" of acculturation appear very similar to behaviors indicative of various handicapping conditions. However, the appropriate and most effective teacher response to many of these learning and behavior problems is to address the students' acculturational needs rather than, or in addition to, the special educational needs. Prior to curriculum implementation, issues such as attention deficiency, hyperactivity, or other learning and behavior problems must be considered relative to the learners' level of acculturation as well as cultural and linguistic background. Effective classroom management cannot occur if these factors are not addressed as instruction is implemented.

Experiential Differences

Experiential differences account for much of

minority handicapped students' achievement below their perceived ability levels. Many refugee and immigrant students in this country come from agrarian populations and, due in part to economic and military turmoil, have not received or been exposed to educational experiences shared by students in the dominant mainstream American culture (Nazarro, 1981; Woodward, 1981). This is also true of many Hispanic and Native American students, especially those in migrant families (Serrano, 1982). Many of these learners are raised in settings with little or no exposure to regular and consistent public school education or various children's educational programs such as day care centers or educational television. As a result, many minority handicapped students lack experiences important for learning in the public school setting.

Differences and deficits in experiential background also affect the minority students' responses to various elements of the curricula. For example, the use of inquiry techniques, behavior contracting, and other individualized strategies are very dependent upon prior experiences. Role expectations and the ability to make cause and effect associations are prerequisite skills often necessary to benefit from these and similar techniques. Thus, lack of these prerequisite skills limits the effectiveness of the techniques. If minority handicapped students demonstrate insufficient prerequisite skills they must be taught HOW to learn in varied contexts and HOW to extract information from unfamiliar stimuli.

Sociocultural Factors

A common sociocultural factor in the special needs of minority handicapped students is the importance of group rather than individual achievement. The relative unimportance of the individual (except as a contributing member of the group) has been documented in many anthropological studies (Barnouw, 1973; Whiting & Whiting, 1975). A person who appears to act apart from the group may be actively shunned or even ridiculed in many Native American and Asian cultures. Many Native American students will try to blend into the group by deliberately denying or concealing their knowledge of a subject (Nazzaro, 1981; Collier, 1983). This has also been observed in Indochinese students (Woodward, 1981). The heavy emphasis upon individual achievement is especially troublesome for some Asian culture students who may already be under great pressure to achieve for the status of their family (Nazzaro, 1981).

Family and cultural expectations can have other effects upon achievement and must be considered in the class management of the minority handicapped students. School achievement may not be a high priority in some sociocultural or socioeconomic groups. This may be especially true in groups where there has been a consistent demonstration that school does not make much difference to the economic, physical, or psychological well-being of the family. The student may place greater emphasis upon expectations in school that directly serve the family and place less emphasis upon school-related issues and tasks perceived as unimportant. The teacher of minority handicapped students must determine the perceived importance of various curriculum issues when problems arise prior to implementing adaptations.

Interaction Patterns

Many cultures encourage more physical interaction and mobility than others. The amount of appropriate touching and proximity to others in both verbal and nonverbal communication contexts varies considerably from culture to culture (Scollon and Scollon, 1981). For example, in most Native American and Asian cultures children show their respect for elders by not giving direct eye contact and by not initiating communication. Certain cultures do not value touching, physical contact, or nearness. Indeed, physical space between speakers and even the length of time between utterances are also culturally defined and related to value systems.

A minority student from a culture that values indirectness and distance as evidence of good behavior may not respond very positively to the use of touching, hugs, and pats as reinforcement strategies. These students may also interpret the use of "time out" in a different way than the teacher intends. Minority handicapped students must be taught when their culturally appropriate behavior is inappropriate in the classroom. This special need can be made part of sociolinguistic and sociocultural survival lessons and should be considered closely by the teacher as classroom management and curriculum adaptations are implemented.

Discrimination

The effects of discrimination upon minority handicapped students must also be considered a special need. Various behavior problems may develop in response to discrimination. It is a useful survival skill to withdraw one's attention from things perceived as harmful and/or hostile to oneself. On the other hand, some minority handicapped students may physically or verbally strike back at situations or people they perceive as discriminatory and threatening. Survival skills learned in coping with life threatening situations of economic or military turmoil may appear as behavior or learning problems within the relatively tranquil atmosphere of the classroom. Again, these may not represent disabilities or handicaps, but rather learned behaviors which can be replaced with other more appropriate behaviors within the context of the classroom.

Cognitive/Learning Strategy Differences

Minority handicapped students also have special needs associated with cognitive and learning strategy differences. Perceptions of cognitive factors such as time, space, number, gender, or colors are all culturally defined and may vary considerably from one culture group to another (Barnouw, 1973). Hall (1983) has pointed out that "time in this sense is like a language and until someone has mastered the new vocabulary and the new grammar of time and can see that there really are two different systems, no amount of persuasion is going to change (his) behavior" (p. 204).

The same holds true for space, gender, or colors. These cognitive constructs are so elementary to one's own culture and language that it is frequently difficult for teachers to objectively separate these cognitive differences from cognitive deficits. Teachers should not assume that what is true in their own culture is necessarily true in another. Even seemingly universal perceptions should be closely examined in teachers' search for cultural relevance.

For example, some cultures do not categorize colors in the same manner as the mainstream American culture (Whorf, 1956). The words for several of the eight crayon box colors have no corresponding term in the cognitive language of many cultures. In Eskimo culture, for example, "orange" and "purple" do not exist. In modern bilingual programs in western Alaska, students are taught to use either "uulincaaq" and "perpelaaq" (Eskimo versions of 'orange' and 'purple') or "qalleryak" and "quisgaq" (words created for items having a similar hue).

Other examples of differences in underlying cognitive structure are gender and time reference. American English and Spanish both have many terms that distinguish gender in the language (i.e., la, las, el, she, he, his). Many Native American and Asian cultures do not have any discrimination in this regard. Words are sexless, and activities in the third person singular (e.g., "x is fixing the boat"), are spoken of as being done without referring to the sex of the one completing the action. This cultural difference will mean that a classroom teacher will need to incorporate some lesson on gender identification and vocabulary when adapting curricula for these minority handicapped students.

Time reference is another example of an area where children from different cultures may exhibit learning and behavior problems as a result of different conceptual structures and cognitive styles. American culture tends to view time as having a reality of its own, as though hours and minutes exist physically rather than as arbitrary culturally defined units. As previously noted by Hall (1983), the way in which people from different cultures perceive time is as varied as the language they use to describe it. One culture's "soon" or "right away" may be another culture's "when I get to it".

Other cognitive differences may exist in the manner in which minority students organize their world and learning strategies. Some cultures appear to view the world as a whole comprised of parts rather than as parts making up a whole. This has been described as "field independence" (i.e., attending to individual elements) and "field sensitivity" (i.e., attending to the whole) and appears to be related to sociocultural differences (Ramirez and Castaneda, 1974). Problems may arise in the classroom if the teacher has a cognitive organization different from or not responsive to that of the minority handicapped students. Cultural differences in cognition have also been noted in studies of cultural bias in tests of cognitive ability or intelligence (Glick, 1974).

Differences in cultural values and beliefs may also affect one's classroom management. Materials, strategies, and settings which work well in one cultural context and with a particular group of students may not be effective with other students. Examples of this can be found in typical English as a second language (ESL) lessons. In many beginning level ESL lessons, students are asked to learn to respond to "What is your name?" and "How are you?" It is considered very impolite, aggressive, and even threatening in many traditional cultures to ask these questions directly of the person, especially upon first meeting them. In many Native American cultures, repeatedly asking the same personal questions is seen as a sign of ill-wishing and sometimes of witchcraft. These and similar cultural values must be considered in order to implement effective classroom management.

Language

Language is the medium through which culture is transmitted from generation to generation and one of the means by which a person from one culture learns about another culture. A particular language is a reflection or mirror of its particular culture. Language development in the primary or native language (L1) occurs within the context of its speakers. The acquisition of a second language (L2) occurs within the context of acculturation. Both L1 and L2 development and acquisition are affected by the acculturation experience.

Language backgrounds may affect the special needs of minority handicapped students in areas such as acquisition and development of L1 and L2, the interaction of L1 and L2, basic interpersonal communication skills (BICS) versus cognitive academic language proficiency (CALP), proficiency in L1 and L2, effect of acculturation upon L1 and L2, and sociolinguistic and orthographic differences. In order to best address these and similar issues, various language-related concerns must be addressed by the teachers of minority handicapped students. These concerns include linguistic background, limited English proficiency, expressive language, and orthography.

Linguistic Background

One obvious language concern for minority handicapped students is that they possess a different linguistic background (i.e., other than English) and yet often are considered to have a language <u>disability</u> rather than a language <u>difference</u>. This was noted by Rueda and Mercer (1985) who reported that speech therapists were involved in staffings, leading to over 80% placement, while specialists in language transition and difference (bilingual/ESL educators) were not involved. Identifying minority students as learning disabled or speech/language disabled learners because they exhibit auditory perception problems in English may conflict with the provisions of PL 94-142. Additionally, this may not lead to appropriate instruction for the students' special needs. Only if the learners demonstrate receptive and/or expressive language problems in both Ll and English (L2) could they be said to have a language disability (Baca and Cervantes, 1984).

Thus, it is important for classroom teachers to familiarize themselves with the linguistic and sociolinguistic features of the Ll and Cl of minority handicapped students. Through this knowledge, appropriate language development can be built upon the students' existing communication skills. Some features of American English may be especially difficult for minority handicapped students given the particular linguistic and sociolinguistic features of their native mode of communication.

For example, sounds that exist in English and not in Ll will be more difficult for minority handicapped students to learn to hear and speak. Sounds that exist in the native language and not in English may appear in utterances in place of similar

English sounds. An example of this is the way Yupik students pronounce words beginning or ending with "g" or "k" in English. Their pronunciation reflects a sound in their language that does not occur in English but that occurs in the same position as "g" and "k". These utterances are not to be treated as articulation errors, but identified as appropriate in one language context and not another.

There are many acceptable and compatible variations of English and combinations of L1 and L2. Indeed, most of us have accents or dialects reflecting our various linguistic backgrounds. Only if communication is severely hampered should the minority students be given interventions more appropriate to speech/language disabled students.

Limited English Proficiency

Minority handicapped students who are limited English proficient (LEP) continue to be tested and taught primarily in English. Sometimes this is because it is not clear to the classroom teacher that the student is indeed limited in English proficiency. The student may have well developed basic interpersonal communication skills (BICS) and appear to speak English. However, as demonstrated by Cummins (1981a; 1981b) and other researchers, proficiency in BICS in English does not mean the student has the cognitive academic language proficiency (CALP) necessary to understand and fully participate in academic activities.

CALP represents much of school instructional and assessment language. CALP must be present and well-developed in minority handicapped students before most instructional materials and strategies can be effectively used with this population. While BICS can be acquired in one to two years, CALP may take as long as seven years to develop, especially if the minority student is not receiving structured assistance in acquiring English as a second language (Cummins, 1981a; 1981b).

In addition, minority handicapped students frequently have limited native language skills as well. This is often the result of parents being told that they should speak only English to their children and allow them to speak only English in the home. As the parents may also not be very proficient in English, this effectively diminishes the quantity and quality of communication and interaction between parents and their children. Unfortunately, all too often, the usual result of this is poor language development in both languages (Cummins, 1981b).

This is an area of significant concern to classroom teachers of minority handicapped students since it has been shown (Wells, 1979) that the quality and quantity of language (L1) between adult and child is significantly related to later school success. Limited L1 and L2 proficiency makes it very difficult to adequately assess and adapt curriculum to minority handicapped students' learning problems, unless nonverbal techniques are used in conjunction with both first and second languages.

Expressive Language

Diminishment in expressive language is a normal stage in L2 acquisition and part of the acculturation process. Students experiencing acculturation and learning a second language progress through a period of heightened receptivity, a silent stage, during which they withdraw from interaction and spend more time listening and observing. This may be misinterpreted as withdrawal associated with emotional problems (Hoover and Collier, 1985). Additionally, in many minority cultures, children are taught to be seen and not heard. This, coupled with a greater emphasis on nonverbal communication within many cultures, may produce minority students for whom it is very unnatural to speak aloud to an adult, especially when answering questions.

This has been reported in Indochinese students

(Woodward, 1981) as well as other minority students (Jones, 1976). Misunderstandings may be created by misinterpretation of expressive nonverbal and sociolinguistic communication (i.e., body language) from both the teachers' and students' perspectives. The differences in nonverbal and verbal expressive communication and the need for attending to sociolinguistic aspects of communication have been well-covered in the literature (Hymes, 1970; Morris, 1985; Scollon and Scollon, 1981). However, this area continues to be largely ignored by the education establishment (Greenlee, 1981).

Orthography

Different ways of symbolizing oral language are obvious cultural differences yet rarely considered when adapting curricula to the special needs of minority handicapped students. Students who have learned to write in a morphologically (i.e., a symbol for each unit of meaning) based orthography may have great difficulty adjusting to a phonemically (i.e., a symbol for each unit of sound) based orthography such as English. On the other hand, Kaschube (1972) noted that teaching learning disabled black students to write morphologically assisted them in learning to read and write English. Kaschube has shown that there may be a greater incidence of dyslexia among cultures using phonemic orthographies than among those using morphologic orthographies.

Minority students may also experience difficulties in direction due to cultural differences. Left to right reading and writing above the line are not universal (e.g., Chinese up and down, right to left; Sanskrit-based systems write under the line, right to left). Thus, cultural differences between orthography may exist and these differences require specific attention to ensure effective curriculum implementation.

Handicap

The third important element to consider when educating minority handicapped students refers to the students' handicaps relative to their cultures and languages. Within this context, it is necessary to ensure that behaviors believed to be associated with a particular handicap are not typical and acceptable behaviors for students in their cultural settings or in the acculturation process. Thus, differentiating between a handicap and typical behavior within the students' cultural and linguistic backgrounds, and the awareness of a culture's view of the handicap are relevant issues to consider as curriculum and classroom management are implemented.

Handicaps and Cultural/Linguistic Differences

The teacher should always remember that many behaviors that suggest a possible handicap may be a normal part of the acculturation process and are to be expected in minority students while they are going through this process. Examples of this include heightened anxiety, confusion in locus of control, achievement below perceived ability, inattention, withdrawal, and problems which appear to be due to cognitive deficits. Students going through acculturation may exhibit some or all of these behaviors at some stage in the acculturation process. If these behaviors were consistently observed in non-minority students, they may justify a referral/placement in special education. When consistently observed in minority students, they may indicate that the student requires special assistance in adjusting to the acculturation process and adapting to the mainstream culture and language rather than treatment for a handicap.

Disproportionate referral and placement of minority students in special education currently still exists. Thus, the classroom teacher may be asked to work with minority students who may or may not be handicapped. If the students' learning and behavior problems are due to cultural and linguistic differences and not to a handicap, then the strategies, settings, and content of instruction should reflect this area of need and not a possibly inaccurately identified handicap.

On the other hand, many strategies appropriate for use with handicapping conditions are also useful in working with any student who has learning and behavior problems. These may be used to good effect with students from a variety of cultural and linguistic backgrounds. The primary concern is that the classroom teacher identify and separate the special needs of the minority student between culture/language and handicap in order to effectively select, adapt, and use curriculum within the total classroom management framework.

Handicaps and Cultural Attitudes

Another important special need of minority handicapped students arises from the differing cultural attitudes towards particular handicapping conditions. Different cultures deal with and treat different handicapping conditions in varied ways. The interactions among students, adults, parents, community members, and professionals will be affected by these culturally embedded attitudes. The family's access and utilization of services for the handicapped, the students' responses to these services, and ultimately the effectiveness of these services and interventions will be affected by cultural attitudes. It is important for the classroom teacher to become aware of these cultural attitudes and values before interacting with either the students or their families. This is especially true prior to staffings; however, this knowledge is a prerequisite for any teacher, student, and/or family interactions.

Some cultures consider certain types of

handicaps to be more troublesome or severe than others. Some react to the presence of a handicapped child in the family by becoming overly protective. Others react with shame and try to deny or hide the presence of a handicap. This may result in not taking the student to receive prescribed treatments or not following through with home-based activities necessary for the learners' success.

In addition to cultural attitudes toward a handicap, the teacher should ascertain how the particular culture deals with learning and behavior problems, and use this information when implementing curriculum. For example, a teacher may use pictures of birds and bird songs on oral/aural language development lessons after learning that in the native culture, the treatment of children with language disabilities involves the use of feathers and bird songs. Thus, this type of knowledge may be useful when selecting curricular adaptation tasks either as something to incorporate into the instruction or as a caution for not selecting certain activities due to cultural attitudes.

Interaction

The interaction of the above three areas of concern (culture, language, and handicap) is another factor in the special needs of minority handicapped students. The teacher should be aware that a handicapping condition will have an effect upon the acquisition and development of both the first and second language and native and second culture as well as upon the acculturation process itself. Each individual case will differ in some way from others. The form of the interaction cannot be predicted, either in extent or degree of effect, or in exactly what way the three elements will interact. The interaction of these areas is explored further in the subsequent chapters through presentation of strategies and interventions.

Chapter 3
Curriculum Adaptation

Not all students are capable of learning
through traditional curriculum and curriculum
strategies. Most, if not all, classrooms contain
students who do not learn without some modifications
or adaptations to the curriculum typically found in
most schools. In many instances, minority
handicapped students with learning and behavior
problems may be appropriately educated within the
regular curriculum if the curriculum is adapted to
meet their individual needs. For some minority
handicapped learners, adaptations of the curriculum
content may be all that is necessary. However, for
many other students, adapting the strategies,
instructional settings, and/or modifying student
behaviors in addition to content is more frequently
required.

This chapter considers the topic of adapting
the four curriculum elements to accommodate the
needs of minority handicapped students with learning
and behavior problems. This chapter includes a
discussion about the need to adapt curriculum in the
schools, a guide for determining curricular areas
requiring adaptations, and an integrative model for
classroom management and curricular adaptations.

Need for Curriculum Adaptation

"Curriculum adaptation" is defined as adapting,
modifying and/or supplementing the curriculum in
order to meet the needs of individual students. The
need to adapt curriculum in today's schools becomes
readily apparent when one considers the similarities
and differences among content, instructional
strategy, instructional setting, and student
behavior needs within a particular classroom. Figure
3 illustrates when the need for curriculum
adaptation exists.

As previously discussed, curriculum content is
often found in a sequentially ordered program
spanning grades K-12. Specific content and
objectives are outlined for students to study within

34

Figure 3
Needs Associated with Curricular Adaptations

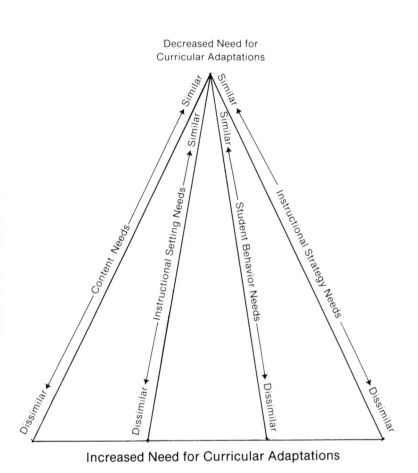

each grade level. The curriculum is designed to provide experiences which developers believe to be appropriate for students at each grade level. Success with the curriculum in subsequent grades depends, to a great extent, upon one's success in mastering curriculum content and objectives from previous grades. Given this structure, the need to adapt curriculum content is minimized provided all students within a specific class or grouping require the same content that is being taught. Therefore, as the differences in content needs among students increases, the need for adapting curriculum content also increases.

Although content to be learned is one area to consider, the other curricular elements must also be addressed. Many events have occurred in the past few decades that have impacted schools and curriculum. One steady and progressive trend underlying these events is the inclusion and education of more students with learning and behavior problems in our schools, including minority handicapped students. This in turn has resulted in an increase in the variability of student abilities in the classroom.

At one time, especially prior to state compulsory school attendance laws, classes consisted of students who exhibited similar needs and abilities. However, teachers in today's classrooms are confronted with many different needs and abilities in their students. As the variability of student abilities and learner characteristics becomes more heterogeneous and less homogeneous, the need for adapting the curriculum elements also increases.

In addition to modifications of content, adapting strategies, settings, and/or modifying student behaviors is also frequently required to meet the needs of minority handicapped students. Thus, as shown in Figure 3, the need for curricular adaptations also increases as student behavior needs, instructional strategy needs, and instructional setting needs in a class or group become dissimilar. The need for curricular adaptations as a result of dissimilar needs is currently wide-spread in our schools and may be seen in many areas.

For example, Hammill and Bartel (1986) wrote that teachers frequently encounter students who exhibit problems in various academic areas. Glass, Christiansen, and Christiansen (1982) stated that a considerable range in abilities is found among students in many classrooms. In addressing this variability in regular classes, Marsh, Price, and Smith (1983) wrote that "regular classrooms will need to expand, reduce, or alter curriculum to meet the needs of each student" (p. 4). Thus, a wide range of student abilities may be found in many classrooms, which emphasizes the need to adapt one or more of the curriculum elements in order to effectively educate all minority handicapped students in our elementary and secondary schools.

Preparing for Curricular Adaptations

The reader should be now aware that curriculum adaptations need to be an integral part of daily teaching if each minority handicapped student's needs are to be effectively addressed in the classroom. Since these special learners are educated in both special and regular education classrooms, special education teachers may be required to adapt curriculum in their classrooms as well as assist regular educators to adapt curriculum in the regular classroom. Therefore, the curriculum adaptation issues discussed in this chapter are applicable to both regular and special education placements. Special considerations pertaining to mainstreaming and curriculum adaptations are discussed in the next chapter.

Curriculum Adaptation Needs of Minority Handicapped Students

As previously discussed, many school districts and/or state legislatures have established mandated curriculum content which all students are expected to follow. Most, if not all, minority handicapped students are also expected to follow, to the extent possible, these sequentially oriented, mandated curricula. For the most part, through administrative and/or legislative mandates, the decisions concerning "what" to teach have already been made for teachers and students. Thus, for minority handicapped students who have difficulty functioning within the prescribed curriculum, the issue at hand is not whether the mandated state/district curriculum is appropriate for these learners, but rather how to best help these special learners acquire that which we are required to teach. Within this framework, curriculum adaptations for minority handicapped students refer specifically to modifying required content as well as adapting instructional strategies, instructional settings within the classroom, and modifying behavior to improve student self-control.

Determining Curriculum Elements Requiring Adaptation

Morsink (1984) discussed three general areas that should be considered when adaptations are determined necessary to meet the needs of students with learning and behavior problems. These included the physical environment, the instruction, and the classroom management. Table 1 provides a "Guide for Curricular Adaptations" that may be used to assist teachers to delineate curriculum areas that may need adapting, once a problem has been detected. The guide has been completed for illustration purposes. The three areas discussed by Morsink (1984) are adapted and incorporated into the guide.

TABLE 1

Guide for Curricular Adaptations

Student: __Tom__   Subject Area: __Social Studies__

Date: ____10-10-86____   Grade: __5__

Length of Instructional Period: __40 minutes__

   I. Briefly describe the classroom situation and task in question:

       Content area addressed during this instructional period:

       ## American History

       Instructional Strategy(s) used during this instruction:

       ## Lecture and Discussion

       Instructional Setting(s) used during this instruction:

       ## Large Group

       Student Behaviors exhibited during this instruction:

       ## Makes tapping noises, looks around room

       Expectation of student during instruction:

       ## Record notes, participate in discussions

       Reason for concern:

       ## Lack of participation, poor grades on weekly tests

  II. Respond to each curricular item relative to the described situation:

       A. Content

           1. Does student possess sufficient reading level to complete activity?
               Yes - Tom reads at a fifth grade level in English (L2) and Spanish (L1)

           2. Has student mastered previous objectives and skills necessary to
               complete activity?
               Yes - successfully completed pretests

           3. Does student possess sufficient language skills, cultural back-
               ground knowledge, and experiences to comprehend concepts
               associated with the instruction? Yes - Speaks Spanish fluently,
               speaks and understands English similar to others in class,
               has been in this school/community since the 1st grade

           Summary of content needs: Tom possesses sufficient reading
           level, prerequisite skills, experience and language background
           to complete activity

39

B. Instructional Strategies

    1. Does selected strategy(s) provide sufficient motivation to student?

       Tom appears to pay attention about half the period

    2. Does selected strategy(s) generate active student participation?

       Tom rarely participates in discussions and records only a few notes

    3. Under what conditions is the selected strategy(s) effective for the student?

       When the lecture is supplemented with frequent discussions

    4. To what extent does the student learn through selected strategy(s)?

       Tom has not learned the material in this unit of study

Summary of Instructional Strategy needs:

Lecturing does not appear to motivate Tom or facilitate effective learning

C. Instructional Setting (one or more may apply to the specific situation being assessed)

    1. To what extent is the student capable of working independently?

    2. To what extent is the student capable of working in small group situations with direct teacher supervision?

       Tom frequently participates in most large group activities during Social Studies

    3. To what extent is the student capable of working in large group situations?

    4. To what extent is the student capable of working cooperatively with one or two students without constant direct teacher supervision?

Summary of Instructional Setting needs:

Tom is usually capable of working and learning in large group situations

D. Student Behaviors

1. What appropriate behaviors does the student exhibit during the instruction?

   For the most part Tom appears to pay attention except when looking around the room

2. What inappropriate behaviors does the student exhibit during the instruction?

   Frequently looks around room and taps pencil on desk

3. During the instruction, how long does the student attend to the task at hand prior to exhibiting off-task behavior? Length of time before returning to task?

   5-10 minutes prior to tapping or looking around, Returns to tasks within a couple of minutes

4. How much of the entire instructional time is engaged in on-task behavior? Off-task behavior?

   50-60% on-task   40-50% off-task

5. What self-management techniques does the student use to manage own behavior and attend to the task at hand?

   Tom is capable of returning to the task without teacher direction

Summary of Student Behavior needs: Tom possesses some self-control abilities. He frequently looks around the classroom and occasionally taps his pencil on his desk

III. Prioritize curricular elements requiring adaptation:

Curricular Elements	Adaptation Priority			
	High	Medium	Low	Further Clarification
Content			X	
Instructional Strategy	X			
Instructional Setting			X	
Student Behaviors		X		

Hypothesis for adaptations: Present Tom with an outline of topics that will be covered during the lecture prior to beginning the lecture. Assign Tom a bilingual peer tutor to answer questions he may have about the content. Periodically stop lecture and ask students (including Tom) to summarize the content to that point.

A self-monitoring program for the tapping noises and looking around may be developed to reduce off-task behaviors if adaptations to the strategy are ineffective.

41

The "Guide for Curricular Adaptations" consists of three sections. In the first section, the teacher documents the classroom and instructional aspects specific to the situation in which the student is experiencing difficulty. This includes what is expected of the student during the instructional activity and the reason a concern exists in that particular situation. This information serves to clarify the existing structure and practices of the instructional period in question.

Section II is completed relative to the information provided in the first section. Each question within the four curricular elements is answered in brief narrative form. The questions in each area are responded to in relation to the situation described in section I only, in an effort to clarify further student needs and abilities within that particular instructional situation. Upon completion of each curriculum element, a brief statement should summarize the responses to the questions in that area.

Section III provides a chart for recording the curricular adaptation priority needs based upon the results obtained through completion of the guide. The extent of the discrepancy between what the student is expected to do and what he/she actually does during the instructional activity reflects the need to adapt one or more elements of the curriculum. Within the curriculum element of content, the extent to which the student lacks sufficient reading level, mastery of prerequisite skills, and language abilities associated with the instructional activity reflects the need to adapt the content. The extent that the activity does not motivate or generate active participation reflects the need to adapt the instructional strategy.

Similarly, the extent to which the student lacks the capability to work in the selected group or independent setting reflects a potential need to adapt the instructional setting. Also, the extent to which a student exhibits inappropriate behaviors, off-task behavior, and in general the inability to manage his/her own behavior within the instructional activity reflects the need to modify student behaviors that focus specifically on self-control. By prioritizing the potential need to adapt each curriculum element the interrelationship among the elements becomes clearer. This is important to consider in order to formulate a hypothesis concerning a proper course of action to remedy the situation.

If upon completion of the guide it is determined that further clarification of the need for adapting the curriculum is necessary, additional evaluation may be indicated. This may include more formalized assessment. The reader is referred to McLoughlin and Lewis (1986) and Salvia and Ysseldyke (1985) for additional assessment information. If further assessment does not appear necessary and curriculum adaptations are warranted, a hypothesis concerning the nature and type of adaptations required are documented.

In the situation illustrated in the guide, the instructional strategy may not motivate or generate active participation and the student engages in frequent off-task behavior. The student appears to possess sufficient prerequisite skills to deal with the content and the instructional setting does not appear to be a major factor. Therefore, either the instructional strategy and/or student behaviors appear to need modifications at this time. The hypothesis for curricular adaptations in this situation should first address adapting the instructional strategy followed by modification of student behaviors in efforts to improve self-control, if the adapted instructional strategy is ineffective. Or, depending upon the situation, simultaneous modification of both student behaviors and the instructional strategy may be completed. The content and instructional setting are not adapted at this time. The hypothesis provides possible alternatives for implementing adaptations to address curricular needs.

Thus, as illustrated in the completed guide, an apparently simple problem may be associated with two of the four elements within the curriculum. Although some extra time is required to complete this guide, time and energy spent focusing on the wrong curriculum element(s) may be minimized through its use. Actual student performances provide the basis for the final decisions concerning the need for and effectiveness of curricular adaptations. Within individual classrooms, curricular adaptations may be a continuous process for some minority handicapped students.

The "Guide for Curricular Adaptations" should be used for a specific student once the teacher has determined that the learner is experiencing difficulty functioning within one or more aspects of the total curriculum. If several instructional periods within the curriculum are affected (e.g., small reading group, math class, independent seatwork during spelling), the "Guide" should be completed separately for each area affected. The guide is designed to ask general questions important in each curriculum element. Additional questions may arise and be considered by the teacher as the guide is being completed. When completing the guide for minority handicapped students, specific attention should focus on the language and cultural issues discussed in Chapter 2.

Class Management Through Curricular Adaptations

Chapter 1 outlined and illustrated the inseparable relationship between effective class management and the curriculum implementation process (see Figure 2). As emphasized, an effectively managed classroom is a direct result of effective curriculum implementation. The most desirable classroom situation for minority handicapped students is one in which the four interrelated curricular elements are effectively implemented.

44

Figure 4 provides a continuum that illustrates further the concept that classroom management and the curriculum implementation process are the same.

Figure 4

Class Management and Curriculum Implementation Continuum

Least Effective	C-M CIP	Most Effective

As shown in the figure, both classroom management (C-M) and the curriculum implementation process (CIP) share a common line forming a continuum. At one end of the continuum the least effective class management is directly associated with the least effective curriculum implementation process. Conversely, the most effective classroom management is directly associated with the most effective implementation of the total curriculum. The most effective classroom management becomes the most effective curriculum implementation process.

Although every teacher's goal should be to remain at the "most effective" end of the continuum, the realities of the various issues in today's schools makes this goal very difficult to achieve even for the most experienced teacher. Achieving and maintaining the most effective classroom management (i.e., curriculum implementation process) for each minority handicapped student in a class presents an even greater challenge when cultural and ethnic issues are confronted. The various factors associated with each of the four curricular elements make the curriculum implementation process for minority handicapped students that much more difficult.

Within the realities of today's public schools

it is virtually impossible to achieve the most effective curriculum implementation process for minority handicapped students without some modifications or adaptations to the existing curriculum that is typically used with other learners. Given the fact that curriculum adaptations are necessary to achieve the most effective curriculum implementation process, along with the idea that classroom management and the curriculum implementation process are one and the same, the most effective classroom management for minority handicapped students can only be achieved through effective curricular adaptations. Within this framework, effective classroom management for minority handicapped students is achieved through effective adaptations associated with the four interrelated elements comprising the total curriculum implementation process.

Figure 5 illustrates classroom management through curricular adaptations while simultaneously emphasizing the importance of considering the interrelationship among curriculum elements prior to implementing adaptations. The lines surrounding effective classroom management are dotted to illustrate the direct impact of curricular adaptations upon class management. Previously, Figure 2 illustrated the influence of the individual curriculum elements upon each other. Just as one curriculum element influences other elements, adaptations in one area may directly affect or are directly affected by the influence of one or more of the other curriculum elements. In essence, one curriculum element may require adaptations in order to accommodate student needs and abilities in other curriculum areas.

For example, content may need to be adapted to accommodate not only student behaviors but also instructional strategies. In another possible situation, the classroom instructional setting may need to be adapted to accommodate a particular instructional strategy. In addition, management

Figure 5
Classroom Management Through Curricular Adaptations

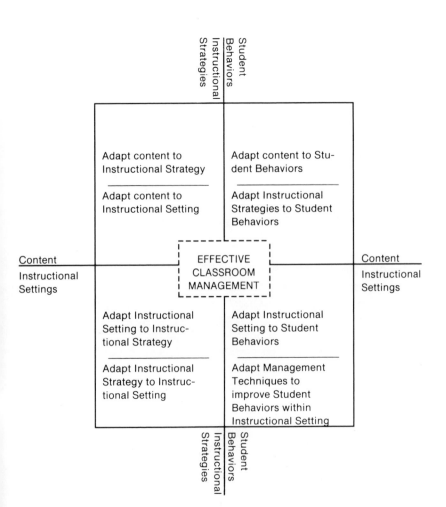

procedures may need adapting to facilitate greater self-control among minority handicapped students relative to specific instructional settings. Additional combinations are outlined in Figure 5.

A concept permeating the education of minority handicapped students is that no curricular adaptations should be implemented until the potential effects of the adaptations upon the other curricular elements have been considered and addressed. The success or failure of any specific adaptation for any one student may rest upon the decisions made regarding the effects upon the other elements. The best formulated curricular adaptations may not have a chance to succeed unless the adaptations are made relative to all aspects of the total curriculum process.

In reference to classroom management, curricular adaptations provide the basis for effectively managed classrooms, which we have seen is the same as the total curriculum implementation process. As teachers consider the management of their classrooms, studying the interrelationship among the four elements of curriculum and their adaptations is crucial. The "situations" (Tony and Maria) presented in Chapter 1 illustrated this interrelationship. Minority handicapped learners who deviate from a teacher's established classroom management require adaptations in the curriculum being implemented. As teachers determine that class management for minority handicapped learners requires change, they need to look no further than the curriculum implementation process for the necessary elements that require modifications or adaptations in order to facilitate effective classroom management for these students.

When considering effective classroom management through curricular adaptations, several learning principles should be kept in mind. These learning principles increase the probability for success with students as learning occurs. Lewis and Doorlag (1983) outlined several learning principles discussed by Carlson (1980). These are presented relative to minority handicapped students. Learning for these students has the potential to improve or increase if the learner:

1. Actively engages in activities designed to address a specific instructional objective

2. Possesses all required prerequisites to the task at hand

3. Practices skills in short periods over longer periods of time

4. Works in pleasant learning conditions

5. Has a program where instructional prompts or aids are gradually withdrawn

6. Is provided appropriate models to imitate when new skills and behaviors are being taught

7. Perceives a system of open communication between the teacher and students

8. Engages in activities that are attractive and novel to increase attention to the task

9. Perceives the relevancy of the material to be learned

As curricular adaptations are determined necessary, these important learning principles should be adhered to in order to facilitate the most effective education for minority handicapped students.

In addition to these general learning principles, other issues specific to each of the four curricular elements must be considered as adaptations or modifications are selected and implemented for minority handicapped students.

Although all of these issues may not be relevant for all minority handicapped students, each should be considered for each student to ensure the most effective adaptations possible.

Content

It is possible to use both L1 and L2 materials in a meaningful manner, either in direct instruction or as content reinforcement. If available, the teacher should obtain materials in both languages, preferably of similar content, and review for CALP level, relevance, and format. Also, it is important to consider the degree of field independence/field sensitivity necessary for the minority handicapped students to use the materials. When considering adaptations to content, the teacher should ensure that the selected material enhances subject area growth without penalizing students for L1/L2 gaps and limited English proficiency. The material should allow for integration of L1 development, L1 to L2 transition as well as L2 acquisition, and be made available in the students' primary language. Material in either L1 and/or L2 should also be appropriate for the proficiency levels in various domains, including vocabulary, syntax, grammar, word attack, and oral paradigms. In addition, the students must possess basic interpersonal communication skills (BICS) in L1 and/or L2 necessary to ask questions about the content, and efforts should be made to ensure that the students do not experience culture shock as new materials and stimuli are introduced.

Instructional Strategies

When selecting and adapting strategies one must ensure that the selected strategy utilizes culturally appropriate cues and reinforcements as well as culturally appropriate motivation and relevance to the minority handicapped students. The teacher should also be aware that some instructional strategies may produce distractions due to unfamiliarity with stimuli associated with the strategy. Teachers must also determine whether field independent or field sensitive strategies are more appropriate and base their selection of strategies accordingly. Additionally, the effects of acculturation experiences pertaining to various strategies must be considered as instruction is implemented for these special learners.

Instructional Settings

Using the setting that is most compatible with the minority handicapped students' Cl should be most effective in the early stages of instruction. The students should be taught how to participate in other less familiar and compatible settings as they become more comfortable with the culture of the public school. The quantity and quality of the verbal and nonverbal interactions that minority handicapped students are involved in are important elements in their cognitive academic development and can be enhanced or discouraged by the teacher's selection of the instructional setting. The teacher must also consider the use of space and time in relation to the students' Cl. Depending upon the degree of experience and familiarity with particular stimuli in the instructional setting, the teacher will need to adapt the manner in which students are introduced to new settings. Additionally, the selection of an instructional setting should consider the student's field independence and field sensitivity as well as cross-cultural communication skills.

Student Behaviors

In reference to student behaviors, it is necessary to consider the interaction of culture and language within the acculturation context and the possible effects of a handicapping condition upon this interaction. Teachers of minority handicapped students should possess cross-cultural communication skills and incorporate these into their instruction. Proficiency in cross-cultural communication facilitates appropriate student behaviors as these skills become effective learning and coping tools in the minority handicapped students' survival repertoire. Developing a sense of familiarity with the school culture and teaching the students appropriate sociolinguistic skills is an important element in minority handicapped students' development of self-control in the classroom. When modifications to student behaviors are being considered, these behaviors must be viewed relative to expected socio-emotional development within the acculturation context.

Although determining the curriculum elements that require adaptations is difficult, the task of actually implementing the adaptations presents an even greater challenge to teachers of these special learners. The careful selection of various teaching and behavior management techniques that will be used to implement the adaptations is the other main ingredient necessary to consider as one creates effective classroom management through curricular adaptations.

Chapter 4

Intervention Techniques

Once curricular adaptations are determined necessary and the special needs of minority handicapped students have been considered, the challenge of actually adapting the curriculum while simultaneously meeting the special needs emerges. The appropriate selection and use of teaching and behavior management techniques form the base for effective curricular adaptations. This chapter describes a variety of intervention techniques that may be used to achieve effective classroom management through curricular adaptations while meeting the special needs of minority handicapped students. We will also discuss several guidelines for regular and special educators to follow when selecting and implementing adaptations in mainstream settings. The issues discussed in Chapter 2 can be effectively addressed if proper selection and use of intervention techniques occur.

Table 2 provides a variety of teaching and behavior management techniques that may be employed to adapt curriculum elements and address the special needs of these students. As shown in the table, several key aspects about each technique are illustrated. They are the process associated with each technique, the desired outcomes when using each technique, an example for each strategy, and special considerations when using each technique with minority handicapped students. Although all of the techniques described in this chapter may be used with any learner, they are discussed relative to adaptations particularly appropriate for minority handicapped students. Some of the techniques and adaptations may already be an integral part of the total curriculum process for some teachers. For these teachers, some of the techniques may not represent adaptations in the strict sense of the word. However, the various techniques and adaptations described in this chapter may be appropriately and effectively used to adapt curriculum to address the special needs of minority handicapped students.

TABLE 2
TEACHING AND BEHAVIOR MANAGEMENT TECHNIQUES

Techniques	Process	Desired Outcomes	Examples	Special Considerations
Learning Centers	Designating an area in the classroom where instructional materials are available for use by students.	Students are able to reinforce specific skills while working at their own pace; individualization.	Create an area in the classroom where several different activities exist for reviewing sight words in both L1 and L2.	The learning center could have visual and auditory stimuli from the students' cultural backgrounds.
Alternate Methods for Response	Adapting the mode of response required of students.	Students respond to questions or assignments in a manner compatible with their needs.	Allow a student who has difficulty with writing activities to tape-record his answers in either L1 or L2.	Ensure that students know varied responses are acceptable.
Individualized Instruction	Designing instruction so individual needs and abilities are addressed.	Learners are motivated and complete tasks appropriate to their needs, interests, and abilities.	IEP may state that student will be able to use particular sociolinguistic cues and responses in appropriate C1 and C2 settings.	IEPs must include language (L1 and L2) needs as well as those for identified handicap.
Shortened Assignments	Providing a student shortened versions of assignments or breaking down longer assignments into several short assignments	Complex or difficult tasks are more manageable to students.	Structure the presentation of weekly spelling words so 2 or 3 new words are introduced and studied each day throughout the week rather than presenting all words at the beginning of the week.	This technique may assist the teacher to check whether students have the preskills necessary for selected tasks.
Providing Success	Ensuring that each student successfully completes assigned tasks.	Improve confidence; student views himself as a successful person.	Initially reduce the difficulty level of material and gradually increase the level of difficulty as easier tasks are met with success.	Must consider L1 and L2 development to ensure success with academic tasks.
Student Input into Curricular Planning	Including students in the decision-making process as general curricular activities are developed.	Facilitate students' ownership in their education.	Allow students to select some specific topics to be covered in an upcoming unit of study.	Ensure that minority handicapped learners know how to contribute in the planning process.

Techniques	Process	Desired Outcomes	Examples	Special Considerations
Role Playing	Assigning students specific roles and creating situations where roles are acted out based upon how they believe their characters would act.	Students learn to confront the reactions of others and ways to deal with situations similar to the role played event.	A specific problem, such as discrimination, is identified and described. Students role play how they would confront the problem and discuss their roles or behaviors upon completion.	This is an effective technique in assisting with the acculturation process.
Providing Choices	Providing students the opportunity to select one or more activities developed by the teacher.	Reduce fears associated with assignments; alleviate power struggles between teacher and student.	Select two different reading selections of interest to the student both of which address the same desired objective. Allow the student to select one of them for the assignment. If student does not select either of these, introduce a third selection and ask student to choose.	Both L1 and L2 development should be incorporated into assignments where choices are provided.
Contingency Contracting	Verbal or written mutual agreement between teacher and student.	Improve motivation, clarify responsibilities, assignments, rewards.	Document in writing that the student will complete 20 math problems with 80% accuracy during the regular math period. Student will receive 10 minutes of extra free time if contract conditions are met.	The rewards for completing the contract must be culturally appropriate.
Modify Presentation of Abstract Concepts	Use of concrete learning activities and simplifying language to accommodate students' current conceptual/linguistic development.	Students are gradually and systematically introduced to abstract concepts.	Supplement the presentations of abstract concepts with visual aids, manipulatives, examples from students' previous experiences, or other direct hands-on experiences.	This is an application of CALP development. The concepts as well as the language of cognitive academic tasks must be taught and built upon students' prior cultural experiences.
Simplify Reading Level	Reducing the complexity of vocabulary and concepts found in written material.	Students study content similar to other classmates but at a level commensurate with their reading abilities.	Provide student with lower level reading material that covers the same topic others are studying.	The materials can be in both L1 and L2 with different reading levels for either.
Peer Tutoring	Students assist in the classroom by working with other students.	Learning gains are experienced by both the tutor and the student being tutored.	A student who has mastered a list of sight words or math facts presents these items on flash cards to another student needing assistance in this area.	If the student needing assistance is limited English proficient, it would be most effective to have the peer tutor be bilingual in L1 and L2.

Techniques	Process	Desired Outcomes	Examples	Special Considerations
Prompting	Providing students with clues or prompts as they complete a task.	Increase the students' probability of generating a correct response.	Underline one letter of a pair of letters that a student is studying, (e.g., 'b' vs 'd'). This helps focus the learner's attention on characteristics of both letters, thus reducing confusion.	Cues or prompts must be culturally appropriate and meaningful to the student.
Positive Reinforcement	Providing feedback or rewards for completing appropriate tasks.	Increase the frequency of appropriate responses or behaviors.	Provide the student extra free time when a math or reading assignment has been completed.	Cultural as well as personal relevance must be considered.
Signal Interference	Using nonverbal cues or signals to control inappropriate behaviors.	Prevent minor inappropriate behaviors from escalating while not providing specific attention to the students' misbehaviors.	Flick the classroom lights on and off when the noise level in the class becomes too loud.	Students experiencing acculturation will have difficulty adjusting to unfamiliar signals.
Proximity Control	Strategic positioning of the teacher or students to prevent or minimize misbehaviors.	Increase students' time on task; reassure frustrated students.	Periodically circulate throughout the classroom during group or independent activities, spending time next to particular students.	Cultural implications of proximity must be considered as personal space varies considerably from culture to culture.
Touch Control	Using touch to minimize misbehaviors and convey messages to learners.	Increase time on task and awareness of one's behavior.	If a student is looking around the room during independent working time, walk up to student and gently tap on shoulder as a signal to continue working.	As with proximity control, the cultural implications of the touching must be considered or the effectiveness of this technique will be lost.
Planned Ignoring	Purposely ignoring certain behaviors exhibited by students.	Reduction of possible confrontations over minor misbehaving; elimination of inappropriate behavior after a few moments.	Teacher elects to ignore some whispering between two students during independent worktime.	This must be done consistently and with equal frequency with minority and non-minority students.
Clear and Concise Expectations	Ensuring that each student is familiar with specific academic and behavioral expectations.	Reduce frustration in students due to unclear expectations; minimize ambiguity in classroom expectations.	Modify or breakdown general classroom rules into specific behavioral expectations to ensure that each student knows exactly what is meant by acceptable behaviors.	Limited English speaking students may require pictures of the expected actions or role played demonstrations of the expectations.

57

Techniques	Process	Desired Outcomes	Examples	Special Considerations
Time-Out	Removing a student temporarily from the immediate environment to reduce external stimuli.	Regain control over self; student thinks about own behavior and behavioral expectations.	Remove a student to a quiet or time-out area for 3-5 minutes when student is unable to respond to a situation in a nonaggressive manner.	Sociocultural implications of the time-out must be considered to ensure students understand the purpose of time-out.
Planned Physical Movement	Periodically providing students opportunities to move about the classroom for appropriate reasons.	Prevent or minimize behavior problems in the classroom.	Allow students to move to a learning center or study booth for part of their independent work time instead of remaining seated at their desks for the entire time.	Effective technique if cultural variations in mobility and interaction patterns among students are considered.
Student Accountability	Ensuring that students are aware of and responsible for their own actions.	Students become aware of the connection between their actions and the consequences of these actions.	Establish rewards and consequences for completing work or exhibiting appropriate behavior, ensuring that these rewards and consequences are consistently implemented.	Limited English speaking students experiencing acculturation may require some role playing, mediation, or other teaching of expectations to best understand accountability.
Self-monitoring	Individual students monitor their own behaviors.	Reduce inappropriate behaviors; increase time on task; students assume responsibility for their own behaviors	Instruct the students to record a check mark on a separate sheet of paper each time they catch themselves tapping their pencils on their desks during spelling class.	This may assist minority handicapped students to learn behaviors appropriate to the culture of the school and classroom.

58

Sources: Brown, 1986; Gearheart and Weishahn, 1984; Glass, Christiansen, and Christiansen, 1982; Lewis and Doorlag, 1983; Mandell and Gold, 1984; Mercer and Mercer, 1985.

Adapting To Meet Special Needs

Based upon the issues discussed in Chapter 2, several educational needs of minority handicapped students can be determined. These include needs associated with acculturation, interaction patterns, limited English proficiency, language development, nonverbal communication, language function, attention to task, concept development, locus of control, perceptions of time and space, and coping abilities. The use of teaching and behavior management techniques with minority handicapped students is discussed relative to these special educational needs.

Acculturation

As previously discussed, students experiencing acculturation may find the learning environment in the public schools stressful and relatively unintelligible. The teacher in this circumstance should use teaching and behavior management techniques which facilitate interpreting and explaining the learning environment and expectations to the students. The techniques should gradually introduce learners to the new element of activity in their environment through demonstration and explanation of the activity or item. As the students become more familiar with one new activity, they may be introduced to another activity. This is related to the observation that discovery learning techniques may not be effective with students experiencing acculturation without extensive demonstration and explanation of the roles, outcomes, and tasks expected of the student.

In many instances the teacher must lead the students through the process, showing them how to complete the task. This is followed by observing the students complete the task and checking for areas in need of further development. Teaching and behavior management techniques appropriate for adapting curriculum to address this educational need include peer tutoring, prompting, providing success, positive reinforcement, establishing clear and concise expectations, learning centers, role playing, student input into curricular decisions, self-monitoring, student accountability, or providing choices.

Minority handicapped students often need to be taught how to behave appropriately in particular settings, as well as why certain behaviors are considered appropriate and others not appropriate. Specifically, the student may need to learn cultural values and behaviors pertaining to proximics (i.e., how close two people stand when interacting in various situations and roles), attitudes toward property and ownership, discrimination, attitudes towards handicaps and status, illustrations of how colors and clothing carry different meanings in different social contexts, and the interaction of sociolinguistic behaviors with other cues to convey meaning in C1 vs C2.

The most basic C2 cultural values and behaviors must be taught first as survival skills for the minority handicapped student. These may include dressing appropriately, recognizing dangerous situations, recognizing to whom and where to go to receive assistance, how to ask for assistance, how to order and eat food appropriately, as well as contrasting similarities and differences between appropriate and inappropriate behaviors, in and out of school settings. Teaching and behavior management techniques for implementing adaptations to curricular elements that address knowledge of cultural values and behaviors include peer tutoring, role playing, individualized instruction, providing choices, contingency contracting, positive reinforcement, clear and concise expectations, and proximity control.

Interaction Patterns

This educational need refers to assisting students to integrate C1 and C2 and to prevent the possibly detrimental assimilation or rejection of C2. This includes lessons in how to communicate without speaking the language, how to participate even when not completely understanding what is going on, the importance of interacting and participating while learning the new language and culture, as well as lessons on multicultural aspects of American society, the pluralistic nature of American heritage, and contributions of the student's culture to American culture and society.

Students should be encouraged to observe others and to respond to them even if they do not fully understand the occurrences. They may also be assigned a peer tutor who will explain the occurrences the student observes. It is also important to teach the students not to hesitate to participate and interact. Students learn to speak by speaking, learn appropriate actions by doing, learn to interact appropriately by interacting, and in turn are interacted with more frequently when they participate. Teaching and behavior management techniques such as peer tutoring, student accountability, self-monitoring, role playing, or student input into curricular decisions may be appropriately used to address interaction needs of minority handicapped students.

Limited English Proficiency

As discussed by Cummins (1981a) it takes one or two years for nonhandicapped minority students who do not speak English to learn basic interpersonal communication skills (BICS) in English. As discussed in Chapter 2, success in BICS should not be mistaken for proficiency in the type and depth of English used in the classroom. BICS should be fully developed as they can assist students to develop confidence and experience success in speaking English as a second language. This in turn forms the base upon which cognitive academic language skills (CALP) are developed.

The teacher should use the students' current level of BICS for encouraging greater verbal communication in English through the use of such teaching and behavior management techniques as role playing, prompting, and by frequently requesting verbal responses in instructional activities. The content, instructional settings and strategies of the curriculum must be adapted to allow and encourage this greater verbal discourse. To elicit more frequent and more proficient use of English as a second language, minority handicapped students must be given more frequent opportunities to use what English they have even though this may only be BICS-level English.

In reference to CALP in English, this may be developed within five to seven years in non-English speaking children in a regular English-speaking classroom setting. This proficiency is crucial to the academic achievement of the student and instruction in CALP should become an integral part of the curriculum used with minority handicapped students. Strategies to use in adapting the curriculum for CALP development also include the use of peer tutoring, role playing, and frequent use of verbal interactions with the students. Students can role play particular school activities and personnel to become more familiar with the language used in these situations. Student accountability and self-monitoring are also useful teaching and behavior techniques as minority handicapped students become more proficient with CALP, but continue to need development.

Language Development

Language development needs of minority handicapped students include L1 vocabulary development, Ll discourse structure and topics, Ll to L2 codeswitching and L2 and Ll codeswitching in planned sequence, translation, contrastive analysis, or transformational grammar. This educational need may also involve revision or clarification, affirmation, acknowledging, commenting, or maintaining a topic in Ll or L2. A variety of teaching and behavior management techniques may be used to adapt curriculum to meet these language-oriented needs. Some of the effective interventions include peer tutoring, prompting, alternate methods of response, role playing, modifying presentation of abstract concepts, providing success, positive reinforcement, contingency contracting, or individualized instruction. In addition, various interactive techniques may be used to develop language skills in Ll and L2. These include mirroring, parallel talk, self talk, verbal reflection, and modeling. The reader is referred to INREAL (1984) for a complete discussion about these strategies.

Nonverbal Communication

Much of expressive communication is nonverbal and minority handicapped students may be more at risk from misunderstandings of their nonverbal communications than for verbal communications (Hymes, 1970). Alternative methods of response, role play situations, signal interference, and peer tutoring which focus upon the nonverbal elements of the communication and situation are effective teaching and behavior techniques to use in implementing adaptations to the curriculum when nonverbal communication skills require assistance. For example, students could act out (without words) the actions of another depicting a particular situation. The "audience" is instructed to generate a description of the situation and provide appropriate verbal discourse. Peers are instructed to cue minority handicapped students when their nonverbal communication is inappropriate or misunderstood.

Language Function

Teachers and students use language, but rarely learn how all the elements combine to achieve proficient communication. This does not mean just talking about grammar or syntax, but how grammar, syntax, or vocabulary function in the totality of communication. When the need arises to assist minority handicapped students to comprehend the function of language and its usage, appropriate curriculum adaptations include use of contrastive phoneme and morpheme (sound/symbol and meaning/symbol) analysis, use of communication with regular patterns, drawing students' attention to these patterns, and teaching how to use these patterns.

Learning centers, modifying presentation of abstract concepts, and self-monitoring are useful teaching and behavior techniques to use when adapting curriculum to facilitate comprehension of language function. In addition, role played situations may be developed where students ask for directions from a person on the street versus requesting something from another family member. This will assist to illustrate the different functions of language as well as how language itself changes in different situations.

Attention to Task

Minority handicapped students will vary in their willingness to work beyond the required time or to withstand frustration and possible failure. A highly persistent student may work until the task is completed and will seek any necessary assistance. A student with low persistence will demonstrate an inability to work on a task for any length of time and/or have a short attention span. It should be remembered that an abnormal persistence (i.e. perseveration) is also a learning and behavior problem. Teachers can use monitored observation to determine what, when, where, and with whom appropriate persistence is occurring. To address this educational need, adapt the instructional setting, instructional strategies, and content to continue to elicit the appropriate persistence as observed by the teacher.

Another facet of attention that should be considered is level of anxiety. An individual's level of apprehension and tension under stress conditions will affect his or her attention to the task at hand. Students do better with challenging and difficult tasks if they are in a low stress situation. Heightened anxiety was mentioned as one of the side effects of the acculturation process and it must be addressed in the instruction of minority handicapped students. Teachers must adapt their instructional setting and content so that stress for the minority handicapped student is minimized as well as use instructional strategies which do not produce more anxiety in the students.

This may be accomplished by using demonstration techniques and concrete cues to ensure knowledge of expectations, teaching students relaxation techniques before stressful tasks, and always prefacing new lessons with a review of previously successful learning experiences. Other teaching and behavior management techniques useful in conjunction with attention to task include planned physical movement, clear and concise expectations, time out, touch control, providing success, prompting, simplifying reading level, alternative methods for response, contingency contracting, or planned ignoring.

Concept Development

This educational need pertains specifically to the ways in which students form and retain concepts.

One aspect of this is conceptual tempo (i.e., the speed and adequacy of hypothesis formulation and information processing). Similar to other students, minority handicapped learners will fall somewhere along the conceptual tempo continuum of reflection versus impulsivity. There exist cultural factors as well as individual personality factors that affect where students fall on this continuum. Some cultures encourage and expect more reflective behavior of learners. Other cultures encourage and expect more impulsive behavior of their children, regarding this as critical to the learning process.

The teacher should adapt the instructional setting, content, and strategies to the current conceptual tempo of the minority handicapped students and use various teaching and behavior techniques to gradually elicit desired school behavior. The culturally sensitive use of contingency contracting, self-monitoring, and role play are effective in conceptual tempo development. It is also important for minority handicapped students to learn which conceptual tempo is appropriate and most effective in a particular setting.

Another consideration in conceptual style is breadth or style of categorization. The broad categorizer likes to include many items in a category and lessens the risk of leaving something out. The narrow categorizer prefers to exclude doubtful items and lessens the probability of including something that does not belong. Cognitive differences are also found when looking at whether students compartmentalize (relatively rigid categories) or differentiate (tendency to conceive of things as having many properties rather than a few). It should be kept in mind that differences in categorization are to be expected between cultural groups (Casson, 1981; Spindler, 1974). For example, students from different cultures may group food items in a variety of ways (e.g., color, time of day used, shape, type of utensil used).

To address these differences in concept development, the teacher must very clearly demonstrate the type of categorization that is expected and, if necessary, teach the minority handicapped students how to make the desired categorizations. As previously discussed, some students may be unfamiliar with different "types" of items (e.g., fruit vs. vegetable, insect vs. animal). These complex categorization skills are common in primary classrooms and are based upon assumptions of culturally similar cognitive understanding of concept formation. Teaching and behavior techniques to use in conjunction with development in this area include clear and concise expectations, alternate methods of response, and providing choices.

When considering cognitive development in curricular adaptations for minority handicapped students, it is important to remember that one of the side effects of acculturation is a resistance to change and new experiences. New activities should always be introduced in relation to previously and successfully learned tasks or skills. Teaching and behavior management techniques useful for this conceptual development include providing success, shortening assignments, or simplifying the reading level of assignments.

Locus of Control

Locus of control refers to internal versus external perceptions of factors such as responsibility, success, or achievement. "Internal" persons think of themselves as responsible for their own behavior (i.e., their own efforts and abilities resulted in success or failure on a given task). "External" persons, on the other hand, view circumstances as events beyond their control (i.e., luck or other people are responsible for their successes or failures). Minority handicapped students may display evidence of external locus of control due to the effects of acculturation. They may also display external locus of control due to continued failure to achieve in school no matter how hard they have tried. On the other hand, minority handicapped students may blame themselves (i.e., display internal locus of control) when failure is really affected by things beyond their control (e.g., their handicap).

Confusion in locus of control may be addressed by the teacher in various ways. For example, students may be taught to remind themselves that mistakes are only temporary, that mistakes help show them where they need to put more effort, and that they should congratulate themselves when they are successful. Other teaching and behavior techniques which would be useful to address this area of need include student accountability, clear and concise expectations, student input into curricular planning, and self-monitoring.

Perceptions of Time and Space

Cultures deal with the environment in different ways. These differences must be considered by the classroom teacher when adapting the curriculum. For example, the teacher may adapt seating arrangements and the time of day for particular activities to make maximum use of the minority handicapped students' particular cultural orientations. The teacher should also be aware of differences in role expectations for males and females and appropriate "personal space." Various teaching and behavior management techniques enable the teacher to develop and teach school-appropriate role expectations within the instructional context, without penalizing the student for school or home differences. Role play, peer tutoring, alternate methods of response, clear and concise expectations are useful teaching and behavior techniques to use as perceptions of time and space require development.

Coping Abilities

The term "coping" refers to an active adaptive process of using strategies to manage one's world (Zeitlin, 1980). Peck et al. (1980) have developed a conceptual approach to coping skills which consists of a series of steps in resolving problems. The classroom teacher can adapt the content, instructional setting, and instructional strategies used in the lesson to develop and elicit appropriate coping behaviors from minority handicapped students. The steps developed by Peck and described by Payne et al. (1980) are confront, engage, initiate, conceive solution, use aid/advice, implement, persist, and achieve solution. Self-monitoring, student accountability, prompting, role playing, peer tutoring, and modifying presentation of abstract concepts are useful teaching and behavior management techniques to use to develop coping abilities. For example, students may act out a conflict situation in the school and discuss ways to appropriately confront the problem. This may include where to go for additional assistance or advice, possible solutions, how to implement the solutions, and how to respond to success or failure associated with the implemented solutions. Peer partners may cue one another as the situation is being confronted and attempts are made to deal with the problem.

Mainstreaming Considerations

If the education of minority handicapped students is to also succeed in the regular classroom, both regular and special educators must be involved in the process. Although the primary responsibility for implementing curricular adaptations in the regular class rests with the regular class teachers, special educators can assume a very important and necessary supportive role in order to facilitate effective class management through curricular adaptations in regular class

settings. Several guidelines for teachers to follow
when developing and implementing curricular
adaptations in the regular class are presented.
These guidelines are presented from the perspective
of both regular classroom and special education
teachers. Special educators should be aware of
guidelines for regular class teachers in order to
best meet their needs and concerns as supportive
assistance is provided. The guidelines for regular
class teachers include:

1. Gather information related to curriculum
   elements requiring adaptations.

2. Consistently implement curricular adaptations on
   a regular basis for a specified amount of time.

3. Briefly document effectiveness of the
   adaptations.

4. Be flexible in your teaching in order to
   minimize problems that may result from changes
   that occur as curricular adaptations are
   implemented.

5. Discuss options for curriculum adaptations with
   other educators, especially special education
   personnel.

6. Adapt only specific areas requiring
   modifications and do not attempt to change too
   much at one time.

7. Continue to try different curriculum adaptation
   techniques until appropriate education for all
   students is achieved.

8. Strategically implement curricular adaptations
   to ensure smooth transitions into the use of the
   different techniques.

9. Anticipate and account for potential problems that may arise from adaptations prior to their implementation.

10. When appropriate, use curricular adaptations that are most compatible with existing classroom structures and routines.

The guidelines for regular class teachers of minority handicapped students emphasize flexibility in teaching and commitment to attempting various adaptations until all students in the class are receiving appropriate education. Given the complexity of needs and issues surrounding the education of minority handicapped students, regular educators must be provided support from educators more knowledgeable in this area of education. The guidelines for special educators include:

1. Assist in gathering and interpreting information related to curricular elements requiring potential adaptations.

2. Assist in the development of materials that require adaptation (e.g., simplifying reading levels of material).

3. Consult with regular class teachers concerning the appropriate use of various teaching and behavior management techniques.

4. Provide suggestions and materials for keeping simple records to record the effectiveness of curricular adaptations.

5. When possible, provide direct assistance to regular class teachers as adaptations are implemented.

6. Be highly supportive of regular educators'

efforts to adapt curricular elements.

7. Provide recommendations for appropriate curricular adaptations that appear to have the greatest chance to succeed, relative to the existing structure in the regular classroom.

8. Assist regular educators to anticipate and account for potential problems that may arise (from the adaptations) prior to implementing various adaptations.

9. When necessary, provide supplemental educational materials to the regular class teachers.

10. When appropriate, recommend to the regular class teachers curricular adaptations similar to those implemented in the special education classroom to ensure consistency in the student's education.

The primary area of emphasis for special educators is to provide supportive assistance to regular educators. This includes assisting in developing or gathering materials, providing suggestions, and in general, providing necessary support as curricular adaptations in mainstream settings become necessary. Thus, as the need arises for curricular adaptations in mainstream settings, both regular and special educators have crucial roles in this process. Through collaboration, effective classroom management for minority handicapped students can best occur in both regular and special class settings through consistent implementation of necessary curricular adaptations.

In Conclusion

This monograph has addressed the special needs
of minority handicapped students with learning and
behavior problems. A procedure for effective
classroom management through curricular adaptations
which address these special needs has been
presented. Intervention techniques appropriate for
meeting the special needs of minority handicapped
students have been described and discussed. Use of
the intervention techniques in adapting the four
curricular elements will result in improved
instruction and effective classroom management for
culturally and linguistically different handicapped
students. Upon completion of this monograph the
authors wish to leave the reader with a final
thought and challenge--the challenge to look beyond
simple solutions to complex curriculum problems
through the study of the interrelationship among
curricular elements, in order to achieve and
maintain the most effective classroom management
necessary to promote a positive learning
environment.

References

Adler, P. (1975). The transitional experience: An alternative view of culture shock. Journal of Humanistic Psychology, 15(4), 13-23.

Baca, L. M., & Cervantes, H. T. (1984). The bilingual special education interface. St. Louis: C. V. Mosby, Co.

Barnouw, V. (1973). Culture and personality. Homewood, IL: Dorsey.

Brown, L. (1986). Evaluating and managing classroom behavior. In D. D. Hammill and N. R. Bartel, Teaching students with learning and behavior problems. Austin, TX: Pro-Ed, 225-293.

Carlson, N. A. (1980). General principles of learning and motivation. Teaching Exceptional Children, 12, 60-62.

Casson, R. W. (1981). Language, culture, and cognition. New York, NY: Macmillan Publishing Co., Inc.

Collier, C. (1983). Acculturation and implications for culturally and linguistically different exceptional children. In J. Bransford (ed.), BUENO Center for Multicultural Education Monograph Series, 4(1), Boulder, CO: University of Colorado, 68-102.

Cummins, J. (1981a). Four misconceptions about the language proficiency in bilingual children. Journal of the National Association of Bilingual Education, 5(3), 31-45.

_____. (1981b). The role of primary language development in promoting educational success for minority students. In Schooling and language

minority students: A theoretical framework, Los
Angeles, CA: Evaluation, Dissemination, and
Assessment Center, California State University,
3-50.

Doll, R. C. (1978). Curriculum Improvement: Decision
making and process. Boston: Allyn and Bacon, Inc.

Eisner, E. W. (1979). The educational imagination.
New York: Macmillan Publishing Co., Inc.

Gearheart, B. R., & Weishahn, M. W. (1984). The
exceptional student in the regular classroom. St.
Louis: Times Mirror/Mosby.

Glass, R. M., Christiansen, J., & Christiansen, J.
L. (1982). Teaching exceptional students in the
regular classroom. Boston: Little, Brown, and
Company.

Glick, J. (1974). Culture and cognition: Some
theoretical and methodological concerns. In G. D.
Spindler (ed.), Education and cultural process:
Toward an anthropology of education. New York,
NY: Holt, Rinehart, & Winston, Inc., 373-382.

Greenlee, M. (1981). Specifying the needs of a
bilingual developmentally disabled population:
Issues and case studies. Bilingual Education
Papers Series, 4(8), California State University,
Los Angeles.

Hall, E. T. (1983). The dance of life: The other
dimension of time. Garden City, NY: Anchor
Press/Doubleday.

Hammill, D. D., & Bartel, N. R. (1986). Teaching
students with learning and behavior problems.
Austin, TX: Pro-Ed.

Hoover, J. J., & Collier, C. (1985). Referring culturally different children: Sociocultural considerations. Academic Therapy, 20(4), 503-509.

Hymes, D. (1970). Bilingual education: Linguistic vs sociolinguistic bases. In J. E. Alatis (ed.), Bilingualism and language contact. Washington, DC: Georgetown University Press, 69-76.

INREAL (1984). INREAL specialist training packet. Boulder: University of Colorado.

Jones, R. L. (ed.). (1976). Mainstreaming and the minority child. Reston, VA: The Council for Exceptional Children.

Juffer, K. A. (1983). Culture shock: A theoretical framework for understanding adaptation. In J. Bransford (ed.), BUENO Center for Multicultural Education Monograph Series, 4(1), Boulder, CO: University of Colorado, 136-149.

Kaschube, D. V. (1972). Dyslexia: A language disorder. Anthropological Linguistics, 14(9), 339-356.

Kerr, M. M., & Nelson, C. M. (1983). Strategies for managing behavior problems in the classroom. Columbus: Charles E. Merrill Publishing Co.

Lemlech, J. K. (1984). Curriculum and instructional methods for the elementary school. New York: Macmillan Publishing Company.

Lewis, R. B., & Doorlag, D. H. (1983). Teaching special students in the mainstream. Columbus: Charles E. Merrill Publishing Co.

Mandell, C. J., & Gold, V. (1984). Teaching handicapped students. St. Paul: West Publishing Co.

Marsh, G. E., Price, B. J., & Smith, T. E. C.
(1983). Teaching mildly handicapped children:
Methods and materials. St. Louis: The C. V. Mosby
Company.

McLoughlin, J. A., & Lewis, R. B. (1986). Assessing
special students. Columbus: Merrill Publishing
Company.

Mercer, C. D., & Mercer, A. R. (1985). Teaching
students with learning problems. Columbus:
Charles E. Merrill Publishing Co.

Morris, D. (1985). Bodywatching. New York: Crown
Publishers, Inc.

Morsink, C. V. (1984). Teaching special needs
students in regular classrooms. Boston: Little,
Brown and Company.

Nazarro, J. N. (ed.). (1981). Culturally diverse
exceptional children. Reston, VA: The Council for
Exceptional Children.

Padilla, A. (ed.). (1980). Acculturation: Theory,
models, and some new findings. American
Association for the Advancement of Science
Symposium Series, (Volume 39). Boulder, CO:
Westview Press.

Payne, G. C., Peck, R. F., Hughes, R., & Breeding,
J. (1980). Cross-cultural study of adaptive
behavior in the classroom. Research and
Development Center for Teacher Education, Austin,
TX: University of Texas.

Peck, R. F., Hughes, R., Breeding, J., & Payne, G.
C. (1980). Coping behavior and achievement:
Validating a conceptual system. Research and
Development Report No. 2433. Research and

Development Center for Teacher Education, Austin, TX: University of Texas.

Ramirez, M. & Castaneda, A. (1974). <u>Cultural democracy, bicognitive development, and education</u>. New York, NY: Academic Press.

Rueda, R., & Mercer, J. (1985). <u>A predictive analysis for decision making practices with LEP handicapped students</u>. Paper presented at the Third Annual Symposium for Bilingual Special Education, Evaluation, and Research, Northglenn, CO.

Salvia, J., & Ysseldyke, J. E. (1985). <u>Assessment in special and remedial education</u>. Boston: Houghton Mifflin Co.

Scollon, R., & Scollon, S. B. K. (1981). Narrative, literacy and face in interethnic communication. In R. O. Freedman (ed.), <u>Advances in discourse processes</u> (Volume VIII). Norwood, NJ: ABLEX Publishing Corp.

Serrano, V. Z. (1982). <u>Migrant handicapped children: A second look at their special needs</u>. Education Commission of the States, Washington, DC: Interstate Migrant Education Project.

Spindler, G. D. (ed.). (1974). <u>Education and cultural process: Toward an anthropology of education</u>. New York, NY: Holt, Rinehart, & Winston, Inc.

Stephens, T. M. (1980). Teachers as managers. <u>The Directive Teacher</u>, 2(5), 4.

Tanner, D., & Tanner, L. N. (1975). <u>Curriculum development: Theory into practice</u>. New York: Macmillan Publishing Company.

Wells, G. (1979). Describing children's linguistic development at home and at school. British Educational Research Journal, 5, 75-89.

Whiting, B. B., & Whiting, J. W. M. (1975). Children of six cultures: A psychocultural analysis. Cambridge, MA: Harvard University Press.

Whorf, B. L. (1956). Language, thought, and reality. Cambridge, MA: MIT Press.

Wiles, J., & Bondi, J. C. (1984). Curriculum development: A guide to practice. Columbus: Charles E. Merrill Publishing Co.

Woodward, M. M. (1981). Indiana experiences with LEP students: Primarily with Indochinese refugee children. Report to the Indiana Department of Instruction.

Zeitlin, S. (1980). Assessing coping behavior. American Journal of Orthopsychiatry, 50(1), 789-798.

About the Authors

John J. Hoover received his Ph.D. in 1983 from the University of Colorado, Boulder specializing in Curriculum/Special Education. He has taught exceptional learners in grades K-12, developed programs and taught at a state-accredited alternative elementary and secondary school, worked as a special education consultant, and served as the evaluator for numerous bilingual and special education programs in elementary, secondary and post-secondary schools. His teaching experiences include work with Hispanic and Native American exceptional learners. He is past president of a CEC chapter, current chairperson of national research committee studying special education teacher training, and has several publications in educational journals. He is currently Assistant Professor of Special Education at the University of Texas, Tyler.

Catherine Collier received her Ph.D. in 1985 from the University of Colorado, Boulder specializing in Multicultural/Special Education. She has taught exceptional Native American learners in grades K-12. She also developed and administered a residential program for severely handicapped Navajo students, a bilingual and special education program for students in Alaska, and a bilingual special education teacher training program. She has authored several publications including several chapters in textbooks. She is currently Assistant Professor, Adjunct, at the University of Colorado, Boulder, and is Director of the Bilingual Special Education Curriculum Training (BISECT) Project.